Born into the Kingdom

The Miracle of Baptism

All of us look a little bit like both our parents. And sometimes we act a little bit like our parents, too.

Draw people that look like brothers and sisters.

Just like we inherit things from our parents,
everyone on earth also inherited things from our
first parents: Adam and Eve.

God said to Adam and Eve, "You can enjoy all the things in this garden! But do not eat of the tree of the knowledge of good and evil."

Sadly, Adam and Eve disobeyed God and did the one thing that He asked them not to.

Just like our actions affect others...

...Adam and Eve's disobedience also affected us.

The good news is that God made a way for us to return to Him by the death and resurrection of His Son, Jesus. Jesus paid the price for our sin!

Jesus was baptized.

We are baptized, too!

When we are baptized, we become a member of
the Church! We have many brothers and sisters
around the world.

Baptism is a grace but as we grow older,
we need to learn to make good choices.

The man flying the spaceship didn't follow his captain's instructions. Because of that, they got lost! He did not make a good choice.

We make good choices by following God's instructions as shown in the Bible and church teaching.

God's church, our family, is made up of many different people!

So even though sin keeps us from God, Jesus' sacrifice for us makes a way for us to come close to God again and be part of His big family!

Isn't Jesus wonderful?